NASCAR RACING

Jeff Gordon

by Kristal Leebrick

Consultant:
Betty L. Carlan
Research Librarian
International Motorsports Hall of Fame
Talladega, Alabama

Capstone press

Mankato, Minnesota

Edge Books are published by Capstone Press
151 Good Counsel Drive, P.O. Box 669, Mankato, Minnesota 56002
www.capstonepress.com

Library of Congress Cataloging-in-Publication Data
Leebrick, Kristal, 1958–
    Jeff Gordon / by Kristal Leebrick.
    p. cm.—(Edge Books. NASCAR racing)
    Summary: Explores the life and racing career of NASCAR Winston Cup
champion Jeff Gordon.
    ISBN 0-7368-2424-3
    1. Gordon, Jeff, 1971– —Juvenile literature. 2. Automobile racing drivers—
United States—Biography—Juvenile literature. [1. Gordon, Jeff, 1971– 2. Automobile
racing drivers.] I. Title.
GV1032.G67L44 2004
796.72'092—dc22   2003014782

Editorial Credits
Matt Doeden, editor; Jason Knudson, designer; Jo Miller, photo researcher

Photo Credits
Artemis Images/Indianapolis Motor Speedway, 5, 6
Getty Images/Robert Laberge, 23; Rusty Jarrett, 27; Steve Swope, 17;
    Vincent Laforet, 21
SportsChrome-USA, cover (portrait), 20; Brian Spurlock, cover (car), 28;
    Greg Crisp, 15
Sports Gallery, Inc., 8, 11, 24
The Sporting News/Bob Leverone, 19

Table of Contents

CHAPTER 1

A Young Star

On August 6, 1994, more than 250,000 fans stood and cheered at the Indianapolis Motor Speedway. NASCAR's newest star, Jeff Gordon, was battling for the lead in the first Brickyard 400. Jeff had once lived in nearby Pittsboro, Indiana. For years, he had dreamed of racing at Indy.

Late in the race, Jeff's colorful Chevrolet trailed only Ernie Irvan's Ford. Jeff pulled his car alongside Irvan and passed him on the outside. Irvan swerved low to regain the lead. The drivers stomped on the gas pedals as they sped down the track's long straightaways. They eased into their brakes as they entered the turns.

Jeff (#24) took the lead late in the 1994 Brickyard 400.

Learn about:

Jeff celebrated in the winner's circle after his Brickyard 400 win.

The two drivers traded the lead several times as they raced around the track. Neither driver could pull far ahead. The race looked like it would have a tight finish.

With five laps to go, Irvan began to slow down. Jeff could tell Irvan was having trouble handling his car. Suddenly, one of Irvan's tires exploded. Jeff took the lead and held off Brett Bodine to earn one of the most important wins of his career. He was only 23 years old.

Jeff's win in the Brickyard 400 was only the second win of his NASCAR career. But it helped start a streak of successes that has made him one of the most famous NASCAR drivers ever.

"... I don't know if any win will ever top that first Brickyard 400. I'd have to say that was the all-time win for me."
—Jeff Gordon, www.jeffgordon.com, 2001

About Jeff Gordon

Today, Jeff remains one of the top stock car drivers in the world. He drives the number 24 Chevrolet. Jeff has won four NASCAR titles and more than 60 races.

Jeff was born August 4, 1971, in Vallejo, California. He grew up with his mother, Carol, older sister, Kim, and stepfather, John Bickford.

Jeff drives the number 24 DuPont Chevrolet.

Jeff became interested in racing at a young age. He was only 1 when John took him to his first race. Jeff began racing BMX bikes when he was 4.

John gave Jeff and his sister a quarter midget race car when Jeff was 5. These small cars look like go-karts. Jeff practiced driving it in parking lots near his home. He soon entered organized races. At age 8, he won his first quarter midget national championship.

Jeff's family thought he had the talent to be a professional driver. When Jeff was 13, the family moved to Florida so he could race sprint cars. When Jeff was in high school, the family moved to Indiana. Tracks in Indiana allowed drivers Jeff's age to compete against older drivers.

Jeff continued to race throughout high school. He graduated from Tri-West High School in Lizton, Indiana, in 1989. The night of his graduation, he was in a dirt track race in Bloomington, Indiana.

CHAPTER 2

Joining NASCAR

Jeff continued his racing success after high school. At age 19, he won the 1990 U.S. Auto Club national midget championship. When he was 20, he won the Silver Crown title for sprint cars.

Early in his career, Jeff traveled with his stepfather to races across the Midwest. The family lived off the money Jeff earned from these races. Jeff and John often slept in their pickup because they did not have enough money for a motel room.

Jeff always dreamed of becoming a professional driver.

Learn about:

➡ **The Buck Baker Driving School**

➡ **Jeff's Busch Series career**

➡ **Jeff's Winston Cup start**

Stock Car Driver

Racing experts noticed Jeff's talent. In 1990, the ESPN TV network made a deal with John. ESPN paid for Jeff to attend the famous Buck Baker Driving School in Rockingham, North Carolina. In exchange, ESPN filmed Jeff's experience to show on TV.

Jeff drove a stock car for the first time at the school. He proved that he was a skilled stock car driver. Jeff believed his talents were perfect for stock car racing.

A year later, Jeff agreed to drive a Pontiac in NASCAR's Busch Grand National Series. Jeff called John and told him to sell all his old racing equipment. Jeff was going to be a professional stock car driver.

"The first time I got into a stock car, I loved it to death. It felt right."
—Jeff Gordon, www.gordonline.com

Career Statistics

Jeff Gordon

Year	Starts	Wins	Top-5s	Top-10s	Winnings
1992	1	0	0	0	$6,285
1993	30	0	7	11	$765,168
1994	31	2	7	14	$1,779,523
1995	31	7	17	23	$4,347,343
1996	31	10	21	24	$3,428,485
1997	32	10	22	23	$6,375,658
1998	33	13	26	28	$9,306,584
1999	34	7	18	21	$5,121,361
2000	34	3	11	22	$2,703,586
2001	36	6	18	24	$10,879,757
2002	36	3	13	20	$7,189,305
2003*	29	1	10	14	$3,920,000
Career	358	62	170	224	$55,823,055

*2003 statistics through 10-1-03

Early Success

Jeff quickly proved that he was a talented NASCAR driver. In 1991, he earned 11 Busch poles by running the fastest qualifying lap. He also won three races. He was named the Busch Series Rookie of the Year.

Winston Cup car owner Rick Hendrick saw Jeff's success. He asked Jeff to join his racing team. Jeff made his first Winston Cup start in the last race of the 1992 season. He was 21 years old.

In 1993, Jeff joined the Winston Cup Series full time. He drove the number 24 DuPont Chevrolet. The Daytona 500 was his first race. He won the 125-mile (200-kilometer) qualifying race before the main event. He then finished fifth in the Daytona 500.

Jeff did not win any races in 1993. But he finished second twice and had seven top-5 finishes. His colorful car and the pit crew's uniforms earned his team the nickname "Rainbow Warriors." After the season, Jeff was named Winston Cup's Rookie of the Year.

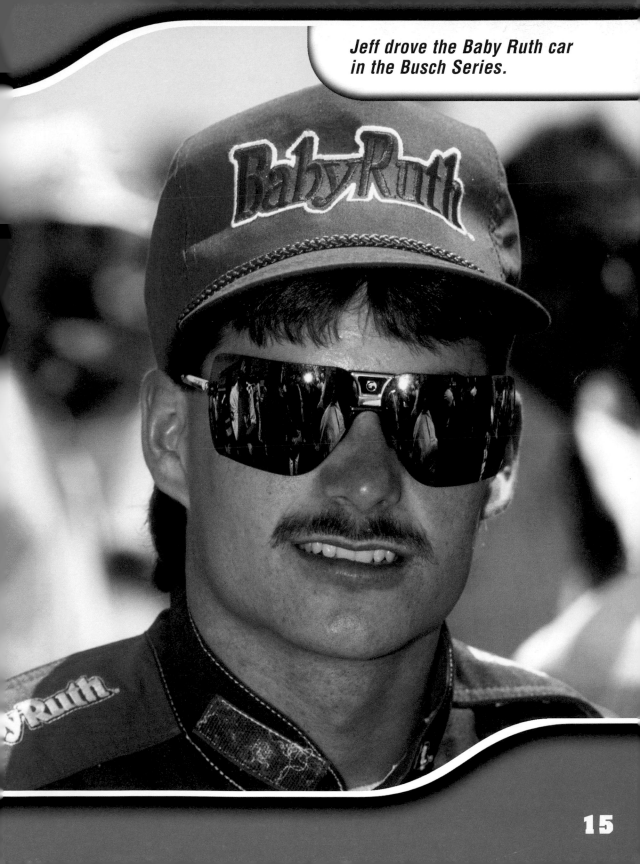

Jeff drove the Baby Ruth car in the Busch Series.

CHAPTER 3

Becoming a Legend

Jeff won two races in 1994. His first win was at the Coca-Cola 600 in Charlotte, North Carolina. After the race, Jeff cried in the winner's circle because he was so happy. Later that year, he won the first Brickyard 400. He was quickly becoming one of the biggest stars in NASCAR.

Jeff earned his first two NASCAR wins in 1994.

Learn about:

→ Jeff's first win

→ A Winston Cup title

→ A record-setting season

NASCAR Champion

Jeff entered the 1995 season hoping to finish among the top five Winston Cup drivers. Few experts believed the young driver could beat NASCAR stars such as Dale Earnhardt and Rusty Wallace. But Jeff proved that he could. He amazed fans by winning seven races in 1995.

Jeff enjoyed his early success. But some fans and drivers disliked him because of it. Earnhardt became one of Jeff's biggest rivals. Earnhardt gave Jeff the nickname "Wonder Boy." Jeff's crew chief, Ray Evernham, thought the nickname was an insult. He asked Earnhardt not to use it anymore. Instead, Earnhardt used it even more often.

Jeff and Earnhardt also battled on the track. In the 1995 season's final race, Jeff clinched the Winston Cup title. He beat Earnhardt by 34 points to become NASCAR's youngest Winston Cup champion. He was 24.

Dale Earnhardt was one of Jeff's biggest rivals on the track.

Jeff crossed the finish line inches ahead of Terry Labonte to win the 1997 Daytona 500.

More Success

Jeff had another great year in 1996. He won 10 races. But he also had some bad finishes. He failed to complete several races. These bad finishes cost him a championship. He lost the Winston Cup title to Terry Labonte by 37 points.

Jeff came back even stronger in 1997. He won the first two races of the year. Later, he had one of his most exciting victories at Bristol Motor Speedway.

With only a few laps left, Jeff was second behind Rusty Wallace. On the final turn, Jeff bumped into Wallace's back bumper. Wallace's car drifted to the outside of the track. Jeff drove low on the track to take the win. Jeff finished the season with 10 wins and his second Winston Cup title.

Jeff had a record-setting year in 1998. He tied a NASCAR record with 13 wins. He also tied a record by winning four races in a row. At one point, he had nine top-5 finishes in a row. Seven of those finishes were wins. No NASCAR driver had ever had such a dominant stretch of racing. He won the Winston Cup title by 364 points.

Jeff dominated the 1998 NASCAR season with 13 wins.

CHAPTER 4

Recent Success

Jeff struggled during the 1999 and 2000 seasons. He won seven races in 1999, but bad finishes kept him from winning another title. His crew chief, Ray Evernham, also left the team during the 1999 season.

In 2000, Jeff won only three races. He finished ninth in the standings. Some experts said Jeff would never be as good without Evernham on his team.

DU PONT

24

MONTE CARLO

Learn about:

➔ **Struggles on the track**
➔ **A fourth championship**
➔ **Car ownership**

Jeff won his fourth NASCAR title in 2001.

A Comeback

The 2001 season began badly for NASCAR. A crash in the Daytona 500 killed Dale Earnhardt. Earnhardt's death was hard on Jeff. The next week, Jeff wore a Dale Earnhardt hat during interviews. He said Earnhardt had taught him how to be a winning NASCAR driver.

Jeff won six races in 2001 and beat Tony Stewart for the Winston Cup title. He became only the third driver to win four championships.

Jeff began the 2002 season slowly. He did not win any races during the first half of the season. But he improved late in the season and won three races. One of the wins was at Bristol, where he again bumped Wallace on the last lap to take the lead. Jeff finished fourth in the standings.

The Future

Today, Jeff is not just a NASCAR driver. He is also a car owner. Jeff and Rick Hendrick own the number 48 Chevrolet. Jimmie Johnson drives the car. Many racing experts say that Johnson reminds them of Jeff. With Jeff's help, Johnson has become a top Winston Cup driver. He finished fifth in the 2002 standings, only seven points behind Jeff.

Jeff says that he does not know how long he will continue racing. He is still a young driver in a sport where stars can have success late into their 40s. He has a lifetime contract with Hendrick Motorsports. Jeff says that he plans to continue racing as long as it remains fun.

"I am trying to find time to enjoy what I've achieved. I realize that my worst day is no comparison to what some people have to deal with in their lives."
—Jeff Gordon, *The Charlotte Observer*, 5-24-03

Jeff is part owner of the car driven by Jimmie Johnson.

2001
NASCAR WINSTON CUP CHAMPION
JEFF GORDON
NASCAR
Winston Cup
Series
DUPONT
AUTOMOTIVE
FINISHES
GOODYEAR

Career Highlights

1990   Jeff wins the 1990 U.S. Auto Club national midget championship.

1991   Jeff wins Rookie of the Year Award for the Busch Grand National Series.

1992   Jeff makes his first start in the Winston Cup Series.

1993   Jeff is named Rookie of the Year in the Winston Cup Series and becomes the first driver to win rookie honors in NASCAR's top two divisions.

1994   Jeff wins his first two Winston Cup Series races.

1995   At 24, Jeff becomes the youngest driver to win the Winston Cup championship.

1997   Jeff wins 10 races and his second championship.

1998   Jeff wins a record 13 races, including four in a row, and his third Winston Cup title.

1999   Jeff becomes the youngest driver to win the Daytona 500 twice.

2000   Jeff becomes the youngest driver in Winston Cup history to win 50 races in his career.

2001   Jeff becomes only the third driver to win four Winston Cup championships.

2003   Jeff starts his 350th consecutive Winston Cup race.

Glossary

crew chief (KROO CHEEF)—the member of a racing team who is in charge of the car and the crew; the crew chief also helps the driver choose racing strategies.

pole (POHL)—the spot at the front of the line at the beginning of a race

quarter midget (KWOR-tur MIJ-it)—a small racing vehicle that looks like a go-kart

rookie (RUK-ee)—a first-year driver

series (SIHR-eez)—a group of races that makes up one season; drivers earn points for finishing races in a series.

straightaway (STRAYT-uh-way)—a long, straight part of a racetrack

Read More

Bisson, Terry. *Tradin' Paint: Raceway Rookies and Royalty.* New York: Scholastic, 2001.

Gigliotti, Jim. *Jeff Gordon: Simply the Best.* The World of NASCAR. Excelsior, Minn.: Tradition Books, 2003.

Johnstone, Michael. *NASCAR.* The Need for Speed. Minneapolis: LernerSports, 2002.

Useful Addresses

Hendrick Motorsports
4400 Papa Joe Hendrick Boulevard
Charlotte, NC 28262

The Jeff Gordon Fan Club
Autograph Request/Fan Mail
P.O. Box 910
Harrisburg, NC 28075

NASCAR
P.O. Box 2875
Daytona Beach, FL 32120

Internet Sites

FactHound offers a safe, fun way to find Internet sites related to this book. All of the sites on FactHound have been researched by our staff.

Here's how:

1. Visit *www.facthound.com*
2. Type in this special code **0736824243** for age-appropriate sites. Or enter a search word related to this book for a more general search.
3. Click on the **Fetch It** button.

FactHound will fetch the best sites for you!

Index